Patterson Elementary School
3731 Lawrence Drive
Naperville, IL 60564

Energy Experiments
Using Ice Cubes, Springs, Magnets, and More
One Hour or Less Science Experiments

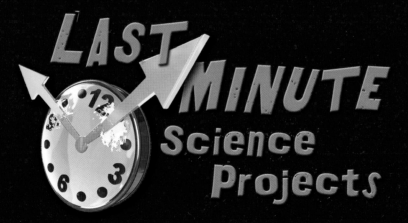

ROBERT GARDNER

Enslow Publishers, Inc.
40 Industrial Road
Box 398
Berkeley Heights, NJ 07922
USA

http://www.enslow.com

Library of Congress Cataloging-in-Publication Data

Gardner, Robert, 1929–
Energy experiments using ice cubes, springs, magnets, and more : one hour or less
science experiments / Robert Gardner.
p. cm. — (Last-minute science projects)
Summary: "Find out how energy is stored, transferred, and changed, what conducts and what stores
heat, and how to change matter from a solid to a liquid to a gas"— Provided by publisher.
Includes index.
ISBN 978-0-7660-3959-9
1. Force and energy—Experiments—Juvenile literature. 2. Science—Experiments—Juvenile literature.
I. Title.
QC73.4.G373 2012
530.078—dc22   2011007629

Future editions
Paperback ISBN 978-1-4644-0146-6
ePUB ISBN 978-1-4645-1053-3
PDF ISBN 978-1-4646-1053-0

Printed in the United States of America
032012 Lake Book Manufacturing, Inc., Melrose Park, IL

10 9 8 7 6 5 4 3 2 1

To Our Readers: We have done our best to make sure all Internet Addresses in this book were active and
appropriate when we went to press. However, the author and the publisher have no control over and assume no
liability for the material available on those Internet sites or on other Web sites they may link to. Any comments
or suggestions can be sent by e-mail to comments@enslow.com or to the address on the back cover.

♻ Enslow Publishers, Inc., is committed to printing our books on recycled paper. The paper in every book
contains 10% to 30% post-consumer waste (PCW). The cover board on the outside of each book contains
100% PCW. Our goal is to do our part to help young people and the environment too!

Illustration Credits: © 2011 by Stephen Rountree (rountreegraphics.com), pp. 9, 11, 17, 19, 21,
27, 33, 35, 37, 39, 41, 43; Enslow Publishers, Inc., p. 15b; Jonathan Moreno, p. 25; Tom LaBaff
and Stephanie LaBaff, pp. 13, 15a, 23, 29, 31.

Cover Photos: All images are Shutterstock.com except for the magnets, © 2009 Jupiter Images
Corporation.

Contents

🎗 Contains ideas for more science fair projects.

Are You Running Late?

Do you have a science project due tomorrow and you've put it off until now? This book provides a solution! Here you will find energy experiments that you can do in one hour or less. In fact, some of them can be done in 30 minutes, others in 15 minutes, and some in as little as five minutes. Even if you have plenty of time to prepare for your next science project or science fair or are just looking for some fun science experiments, you can enjoy this book, too.

Most of the experiments are followed by a "Keep Exploring" section. There you will find ideas for projects or experiments in which the details are left to you. You can design and carry out your own experiments, **under adult supervision**, when you have more time.

Sometimes you may need a partner. Work with someone who likes to experiment as much as you do so you will both have fun. Please follow any safety warnings and work with an adult when it is suggested.

This is a book about energy, and energy is related to work. So you need to know how a scientist defines work. To a scientist, work is a force times a distance. If you lift a 10-pound weight to a height of 3 feet, you do 30 foot-pounds of work because:

$$10 \text{ lbs x } 3 \text{ ft} = 30 \text{ ft-lbs.}$$

If you are using the metric system and lift a 10-newton weight through a height of 2 meters, the work you do is 20 newton-meters because:

$$10 \text{ N x } 2 \text{ m} = 20 \text{ N-m, or } 20 \text{ joules.}$$

The Scientific Method

Different sciences use different ways of experimenting. Depending on the problem, one method is likely to be better than another. Designing a new medicine for heart disease and finding evidence of water on Mars require different experiments.

Even with these differences, most scientists use the scientific method. This includes: making an observation, coming up with a question, making a hypothesis (a possible answer to the question) and a prediction (an if-then statement), designing and conducting an experiment, analyzing results, drawing conclusions, and deciding if the hypothesis is true or false. Scientists share their results. They publish articles in science journals.

Once you have a question, you can make a hypothesis. Your hypothesis is a possible answer to the question (what you think will happen). For example, you might hypothesize that doing work on metal can create heat.

In most cases you should do a controlled experiment. This means having two groups that are treated the same except for the thing being tested. That thing is called a variable. To test the hypothesis above, you might have two weights each connected to a fishing line wrapped around an aluminum cylinder a meter above a floor. A thermometer in each aluminum cylinder could measure temperature. You would let one weight fall to the floor doing work on the cylinder. You would see the temperature of the cylinder rise as the fishing line rubs on the aluminum. The other cylinder's temperature would not change. You would say that your hypothesis is true.

The results of one experiment often lead to another question. Or they may send you off in another direction. Whatever the results, something can be learned from every experiment!

Science Fairs

All of the investigations in this book contain ideas that might lead you to a science fair project. However, judges at science fairs do not reward projects or experiments that are simply copied from a book. For example, a diagram of a steam engine would not impress most judges; however, a unique method of showing that energy is conserved would be likely to gain their attention.

Science fair judges tend to reward creative thought and imagination. It is difficult to be creative or imaginative unless you are really interested in your project. Therefore, try to choose an investigation that excites you. And before you jump into a project, consider, too, your own talents and the cost of the materials you will need.

If you decide to use an experiment or idea found in this book for a science fair, find ways to modify or extend it. This should not be difficult. As you do investigations, you will get new ideas. You will think of questions that experiments can answer. The experiments will make great science fair projects because the ideas are your own and are interesting to you.

Your Notebook

Your notebook, as any scientist will tell you, is a valuable possession. It should contain ideas you may have as you experiment, sketches you may draw, calculations you make, and hypotheses you may suggest. It should include a description of every experiment you do, the data you record, such as voltages, currents, resistors, weights, and so on. It should also contain the results of your experiments, graphs you draw, and any conclusions you may be able to reach based on your results.

Safety First

1. Do any experiments or projects, whether from this book or of your own design, under the adult supervision of a science teacher or other knowledgeable adult.

2. Read all instructions carefully before proceeding with a project. If you have questions, check with your supervisor before going any further.

3. Always wear safety goggles when doing experiments that could cause particles to enter your eyes. Tie back long hair and wear shoes that cover your feet completely.

4. Do not eat or drink while experimenting. Never taste substances being used (unless instructed to do so).

5. Never let water droplets come in contact with a hot lightbulb.

6. Never experiment with household electricity. Instead, use batteries.

7. Use only alcohol-based thermometers. Older thermometers may contain mercury, which is a dangerous substance. If you have a mercury thermometer in the house, ask an adult if it can be taken to a local thermometer exchange location.

8. Maintain a serious attitude while conducting experiments.

9. At the end of every activity, clean all materials used and put them away. Then wash your hands thoroughly with soap and water.

One Hour or Less

Here are energy experiments that you can do in one hour or less. You don't have any time to lose, so let's get started!

1 Finding Changes in the Kind of Energy

What's the Plan?

Let's see how energy changes from one form to another.

What You Do

1. Place a Super Ball™ on a smooth wood, tile, or concrete floor. Lift the ball to a height of one meter or one yard. You did work on the ball. You gave it potential energy due to gravity (PEG).

2. Drop the ball from the raised height. Have a partner watch and record its bounce height (Figure 1a).

3. As it hit the floor, the ball was squeezed together, giving it elastic potential energy (EPE).

4. To see that the ball was squeezed, spread some white flour on the floor.

5. Drop the ball so it hits the flour. Catch the ball after it bounces.

WHAT YOU NEED:

- black or colored Super Ball™
- smooth wood, tile, or concrete floor
- meter or yardstick
- a partner
- pen or pencil
- notebook
- white flour

6. Examine the ball. You will see a circle of flour marking the part of the ball that was compressed, giving it EPE (Figure 1b).

7. Drop the ball again. Let it bounce until it stops.

What's Going On?

The falling ball lost PEG. It gained motion energy, also called kinetic energy (KE). Upon hitting the floor, it was squeezed together like a compressed spring. Its KE changed to EPE. After rebounding, its EPE changed to KE. As it rose, it lost KE while gaining PEG. Its rebound height was less than the height from which you dropped it (Figure 1c). That missing energy exists as a small amount of thermal (heat) energy in the floor and ball. After it stops bouncing, all the PEG you gave it has changed to thermal (heat) energy in the floor and ball.

Keep Exploring—If You Have More Time!

- Try dropping other balls (tennis, baseball, basketball, etc.). Measure their rebound height. Which ball loses the most energy to heat? The least?

- Do an experiment to see if the ball's temperature affects its bounce height.

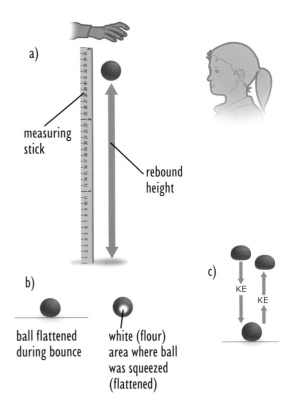

a) measuring stick

rebound height

b) ball flattened during bounce

white (flour) area where ball was squeezed (flattened)

c) KE   KE

Figure 1. a) Measure the height to which a Super Ball bounces. b) Measure the area over which the ball is compressed as kinetic energy is changed to elastic potential energy. c) A diagram of the energy changes in this experiment.

2 Finding the Energy (Heat) to Melt One Gram of Ice

What's the Plan?

Let's find the heat needed to melt one gram of ice.

What You Do

1. Measure 100 mL (100 g) of water at about 30°C (86°F) into a graduated cylinder. Pour into a foam cup. (Remember: 1 mL of water weighs 1 g.)

2. Wipe an ice cube with a paper towel.

3. Add the ice to the water (Figure 2). Stir with a thermometer. If necessary, quickly add more small pieces of ice you have dried until the water is approximately 10°C (50°F).

4. Pour the water, which contains the melted ice, into the graduated cylinder. Subtract 100 mL from the present volume to find how much ice melted.

What's Going On?

The heat lost by the warm water equals the water's mass (100 g) times its change in temperature. Suppose the temperature change of the water was: 30°C − 10°C = 20°C. How much heat did the 100 g of water lose? Since 100 g x 20°C = 2,000 cal, the water lost 2,000 calories.

The heat lost by the water did two things: (1) It melted the ice, and (2) It warmed the melted ice from 0°C (the melting temperature of ice) to the water's final temperature.

Suppose the final volume of water was 122 mL. That would mean 22 g of ice melted (122 g − 100 g). The heat to warm the melted ice from 0° to 10°C was 22 g x 10°C = 220 cal. The remaining 1,780 calories (2,000 − 220) were used to melt the ice. According to this example, the heat to melt one gram of ice was 1,780 cal / 22 g = 81 cal/g.

Keep Exploring—If You Have More Time!

- Why were you asked to adjust water temperatures above and below room temperature? Explain using experiments.

Figure 2. An experiment to find out how much heat, in calories, is needed to melt one gram of ice. A calorie (cal) is the amount of heat needed to raise the temperature of one gram (g) of water through one degree Celsius (1°C).

3 Finding the Energy Stored in Candle Wax

What's the Plan?

Let's find the energy stored in one gram of candle wax.

What You Do

1. Weigh a short candle. Record its mass.

2. Put the candle in a short candle holder (Figure 3).

3. Using a can opener, remove the bottom from a large (28–36 oz), empty can.

4. Using a small can opener, cut 6 triangular openings around the can's base.

5. Using a paper punch, make two holes, on opposite sides, near the top of an empty 6-ounce frozen juice can. Insert a stick or long nail through the holes. Rest the smaller can on the large can.

6. Lift the large can. Put the candle under the small juice can.

7. Add 100 mL (100 g) of cold water (10 to 15°C below room temperature) to the small can.

WHAT YOU NEED:

- an adult
- short, used candle
- balance that can record ± 0.1 g or, better, 0.01g
- small candle holder
- can opener
- 28- to 36-oz empty can
- small can opener
- paper punch
- 6-oz frozen juice can
- stick or long nail
- cold water 10 to 15°C below room temperature
- alcohol or digital based thermometer
- matches
- pencil and notebook

8. Using a thermometer, measure and record the water's temperature.

9. Lift the two cans. Ask an adult to light the candle. Replace the cans over the burning candle. The top of the flame should just touch the bottom of the smaller can.

10. Stir the water with the thermometer. When the water temperature is 10 to 15°C above room temperature, blow out the candle. Stir and record the final temperature.

11. Reweigh and record the candle's mass.

What's Going On?

From the data, you can find the approximate energy stored in one gram of candle wax. (The oxygen added a little energy as it combined with wax during burning.)

For example, suppose the water's temperature rose 25°C, from 10°C to 35°C. Then the heat delivered to the 100 g of water was 2,500 calories because: 100 g x 25°C = 2,500 cal.

If the candle lost 0.40 grams, the energy per gram in the candle wax was 6,300 cal/g because: 2,500 cal/ 0.40 g = 6,300 cal/g.

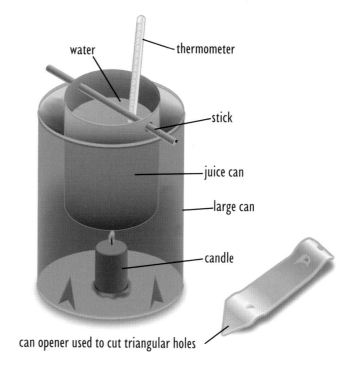

water — thermometer

stick

juice can

large can

candle

can opener used to cut triangular holes

Figure 3. Put a small or well used candle in a small candle holder. Use a small can opener to make triangular holes around the base of the can.

4 The Energy Stored in a Spring

What's the Plan?

Let's see how a spring stretches when work is done on it.

What You Do

1. Hang a spring from a firm hook.

2. Use a clamp or tape to fasten a meterstick beside the spring, as shown in Figure 4a. Use the meterstick to measure how much the spring stretches when pulled by weights. A clothespin on the meterstick can be used to mark the spring's stretch.

3. Add masses to the spring in 0.5 kg increments—0.5, 1.0, 1.5, etc.

4. Measure and record the amount the spring is stretched by each mass hanging on the spring.

5. Use your data to plot a graph (Figure 4b) of the force on the spring, in newtons, vs. the amount the spring is stretched, in meters. (One kilogram weighs nearly 10 newtons.) Use a ruler to draw a line through the data points.

What's Going On?

From the straight line graph, you can see that the spring's stretch is proportional to the force that did work on the spring. This relationship is known as Hooke's Law. The slope of the graph has the units N/m. It is called the spring constant. The area under the graph at any amount of stretch equals the work done on the spring or the energy stored in the spring.

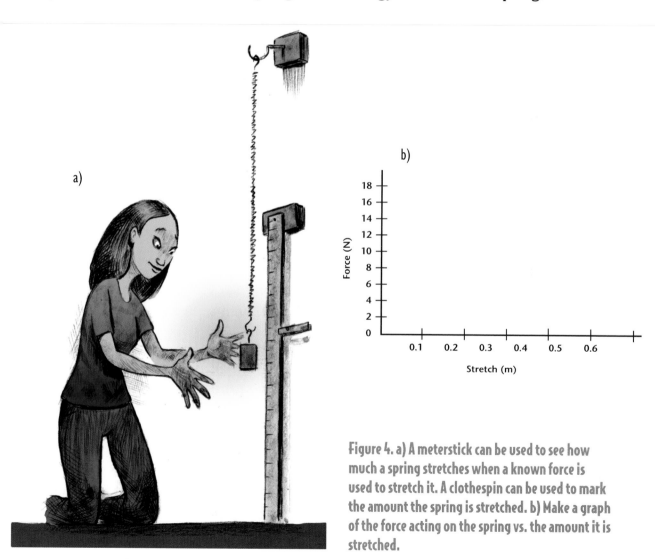

Figure 4. a) A meterstick can be used to see how much a spring stretches when a known force is used to stretch it. A clothespin can be used to mark the amount the spring is stretched. b) Make a graph of the force acting on the spring vs. the amount it is stretched.

5 Giving a Basketball Kinetic Energy

What's the Plan?

Let's measure the kinetic energy you give a basketball. Kinetic energy is an object's energy of motion. It is equal to one half of the object's mass times its velocity squared ($1/2\ mv^2$). A basketball's mass is 0.6 kg.

WHAT YOU NEED:

- basketball court
- basketball
- a partner
- stopwatch
- tape measure
- notebook and pencil
- masking tape
- calculator (optional)

What You Do

1. Stand at the end line of a basketball court holding a basketball. Have a partner with a stopwatch stand on a sideline (Figure 5).

2. Throw the ball with a horizontal velocity. Your partner should start the stopwatch when the ball leaves your hand. He or she should stop the watch when the ball strikes the floor and mark the point with tape where the ball lands.

3. Measure the distance the ball traveled with a tape measure.

4. Find the ball's velocity. Divide the distance it traveled by the time on the stopwatch. For example, if the ball traveled 15 meters in 0.75 second, its velocity was:

$$15\ m\ /\ 0.75\ s\ =\ 20\ m/s.$$

Its kinetic energy would be:

$$KE = 1/2\ mv^2 = 1/2 \times 0.60\ kg \times (20\ m/s)^2 = 120\ \text{joules or newton-meters.}$$

What's Going On?

You did work on the ball. You applied a force to the ball over the distance your arm moved. (Remember: work = force x distance.) That work gave the ball kinetic energy.

Keep Exploring—If You Have More Time!

- From a basketball's kinetic energy, you know how much work you did on it. Experiment to find the average force you exert on the ball as you throw it.

- At what angle should you throw a ball to make it travel the greatest distance?

- How much kinetic energy can you develop when you run?

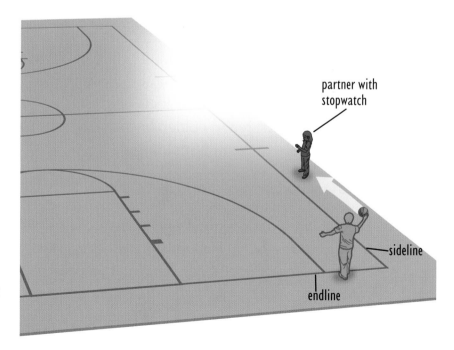

Figure 5. Measuring the kinetic energy of a basketball

17

30 Minutes or Less

Really pressed for time? Here are some experiments you can do in 30 minutes or less.

6 How Fast Does Heat Move?

What's the Plan?

Let's find out whether or not heat moves better in some kinds of matter than in others.

What You Do

1. Place a wooden bowl, a glass bowl, and a metal bowl on a counter. Be sure they all came from the same room so they are all at the same temperature.

2. Put your hand on each of the bowls in turn (Figure 6). The metal feels coldest. Of course, it is not really colder because all of the bowls are at room temperature.

3. Fill the wooden, glass, and metal bowls with hot tap water.

4. Empty the wooden bowl and turn it over. Place your hand on the dry bottom of the bowl. Repeat the procedure for the metal and glass bowls. You will feel the metal conduct heat to your hand better than the glass or wood.

5. Place a metal pan and a wooden cutting board in a freezer.

WHAT YOU NEED:

- wooden, glass, and metal bowls
- clock or watch
- hot tap water
- metal pan
- wooden cutting board
- freezer

18

6. After about 20 minutes, remove them. Hold one in each hand. You can feel heat being conducted from your hand to the metal faster than to the wood.

What's Going On?

Thermal energy (heat) moves through matter because of the motion of particles (molecules, and in metals, electrons). Particles move faster at higher temperatures than at lower temperatures. Fast-moving particles bump into slower particles and transfer some of their energy to the slower ones. In this way, heat moves through matter. It is called heat conduction. The greater the thermal conductivity of a substance, the faster heat flows through it. Metal conducts heat better than glass. Glass conducts heat better than wood.

Keep Exploring—If You Have More Time!

- Does the shape of a piece of ice affect the rate at which it melts? Do experiments to find out. Then explain your results.

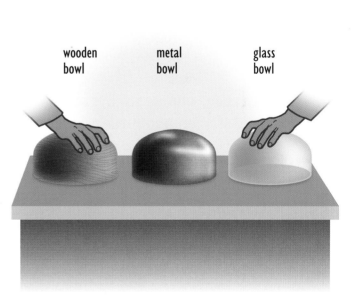

wooden bowl   metal bowl   glass bowl

Figure 6. Which type of matter—metal, wood, or glass—is the best heat conductor?

7 Finding Heat Conductors and Insulators

What's the Plan?

Let's find good and poor heat conductors. Poor conductors are also known as insulators.

What You Do

1. Fill a large basin to a depth of about 5 cm (2 in) with a mixture of ice and cold tap water.

2. Half fill a metal can with hot tap water. Measure and record the hot water's temperature with a thermometer.

3. Put the can of hot water into the ice water (Figure 7). Measure the temperature of the hot water every minute until it reaches 10°C (50°F). Record the temperatures and times in a table.

4. Repeat the experiment using a glass jar with the same amount of hot water at the same initial temperature.

5. Perform the experiment a third time with the hot water in a foam cup.

6. Plot a graph of temperature versus time for each container. Plot all three sets of data on the same graph.

WHAT YOU NEED:

- large basin
- ice
- cold water
- ruler
- metal can
- hot water
- thermometer
- pen or pencil
- notebook
- clock or watch with second hand
- glass jar
- foam cup
- graph paper

20

7. Examine the graph's three curves.

What's Going On?

The metal can is the best conductor. Water cooled fastest in it because it is the best conductor. Water cooled slowest in the foam cup. It's the best insulator.

Keep Exploring—If You Have More Time!

- Put 100 mL of hot tap water into five different containers—a tin can, a paper cup, a plastic cup, a foam cup, and a foam cup with a foam cup cover. (The cover should have a hole so that a thermometer can go through it.) Place all five cups side by side. Measure the temperature in each cup at two-minute intervals. Plot temperature vs. time for each cup on the same graph.

  In which cup did the water cool fastest? Slowest? Which material is the best insulator? Does a cover affect the rate at which a liquid cools?

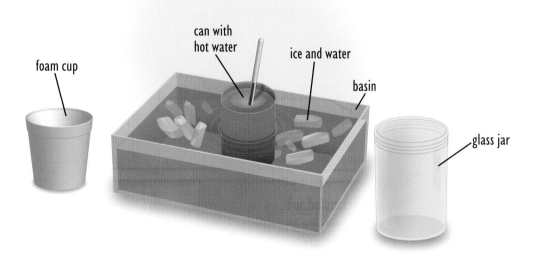

Figure 7. Which conducts heat fastest, a tin (steel) can, a glass jar, or a foam cup?

8 Transferring Energy

What's the Plan?

Let's see how energy can be transferred from one pendulum to another.

What You Do

1. Using string, masking tape, and two heavy steel washers or, better, lead fishing sinkers, build two pendulums. The pendulums should both be the same length [about 30 cm (12 inches)] from edge of counter to center of washers or sinkers. The pendulums should be about 15 cm (6 in) apart.

2. Pull the bob (washer or sinker) of one pendulum back one or two inches and let it go. Watch its potential energy change to kinetic (motion) energy and then back to potential over and over as it swings back and forth.

3. Connect the two pendulums with a stick about one-third of the way from the counter to the bobs (Figure 8).

4. When both bobs are at rest, pull one bob back an inch or two and release it. Notice how energy is transferred back and forth between the two pendulums.

What's Going On?

The stick connecting the pendulums allows one pendulum to push on the other and transfer its kinetic energy.

Keep Exploring—If You Have More Time!

- If the pendulums are of different lengths, can all the energy be transferred?

- Do experiments to find out: (a) How the length of a pendulum affects its period (the time to swing back and forth once). (b) How the weight of the bob affects a pendulum's period. (c) How the distance that the bob swings (its amplitude) affects its period.

Figure 8. Build two pendulums each about 30 cm (12 in) long. Use a stick to connect the pendulums.

9 Checking the Wattage of an Immersion Heater

What's the Plan

Let's check the wattage of an immersion heater.

What You Do

1. Record the wattage written on an immersion heater. [1 watt = 0.24 calorie/second (cal/s).]

2. Add an ice cube to a glass of water. Stir with a thermometer until the water temperature is 8 to 10°C (14–18°F) below room temperature.

3. Measure out 100 mL of the cold water by pouring it into a graduated cylinder or metric measuring cup. Remember: 1 mL of water weighs 1 gram and 1 calorie is the heat needed to raise the temperature of 1 gram of water 1°C.

4. Pour the cool water into a foam (insulated) cup. Measure and record the temperature of the cool water.

5. Put the immersion heater into the cup of cool water. Ask an adult to plug the heater into an electrical outlet while you hold the cup (Figure 9).

WHAT YOU NEED:

- an adult
- immersion heater
- notebook
- pen or pencil
- ice cube
- glass of cold water
- thermometer (-20 to 50°C)
- graduated cylinder or metric measuring cup
- foam (insulated) cup
- electrical outlet
- watch or clock with second hand
- calculator (optional)

6. After exactly 30 seconds, ask the adult to unplug it. Leave the heater in the water.

7. Stir the water with the thermometer until the temperature stops rising. Record the final temperature of the water.

What's Going On?

The heat, in calories, transferred to the water was:

100 g times the water's change in temperature. (Equation 1.)

The heat, in calories, you would expect from the heater would be:

The wattage written on the heater x 0.24 cal/s x 30 s. (Equation 2.)

If the wattage written on the heater is correct, equations 1 and 2 should be very nearly equal. Is the wattage on your heater reasonably accurate? If not, what do you think it should be?

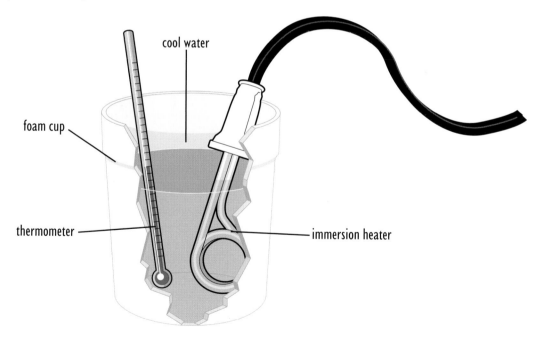

cool water

foam cup

thermometer

immersion heater

Figure 9. Is your immersion heater's wattage rating correct? If not, what should it be?

15 Minutes or Less

Time is really in short supply if you need an experiment you can do in 15 minutes. Here to rescue you are four more experiments you can do quickly.

10 Do Solids Expand When Heated?

What's the Plan?

Let's see if solids expand (enlarge) when heated.

What You Do

1. Use a hammer to drive an aluminum nail through the bottom of an empty tin can (Figure 10a).

2. Remove the nail. Make sure the nail fits through the hole you made.

3. Put on an oven mitt and hold the nail with pliers. Then, **under adult supervision**, heat the aluminum nail in the flame of a bunsen burner or a gas stove (Figure 10b).

4. When you are sure the nail is very hot, continue holding it with pliers. Quickly try to move it through the hole in the can (Figure 10c). You will find it is too large to fit through the hole.

5. Let the nail cool. When cool, it will fit through the hole.

> **WHAT YOU NEED:**
> - an adult
> - hammer
> - aluminum nail
> - clean, empty tin can
> - aluminum nail pliers
> - matches
> - bunsen burner or gas stove
> - oven mitt

What's Going On?

Most substances expand when heated. Heated molecules move faster and take up slightly more space than cooler ones. The aluminum nail expanded when you heated it. Its diameter became larger than the diameter of the hole it made when it was colder.

Keep Exploring—If You Have More Time!

- Do an experiment to show that water, unlike other substances, expands when it freezes.

- Engineers must take heat expansion into account when many things are built. For example, steel railroad tracks have gaps between them. The gaps account for the "clickety-clack" you hear when train wheels roll over them. Where else can you find evidence that expansion due to rising temperatures has been allowed for?

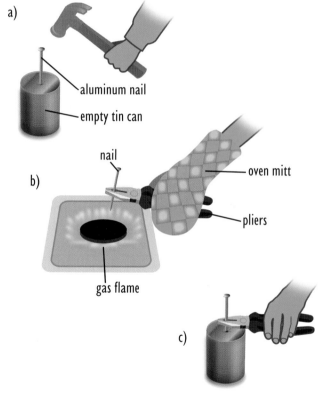

Figure 10. a) Drive an aluminum nail through the bottom of an empty tin can. b) Heat the nail in a hot flame. c) Does the hot nail still fit through the hole?

11 Changing Magnetic Potential Energy to Kinetic Energy

What's the Plan?

Let's see if we can change magnetic potential energy into kinetic (motion) energy.

WHAT YOU NEED:

- 2 bar magnets with poles marked N and S
- heavy books
- table
- thread
- paper clip
- tape
- scissors

What You Do

1. On a table top, push the north poles of two bar magnets close together. You will feel a repelling force.

2. Release one of the magnets. It moves away from the other magnet. It has kinetic energy. It stops only because the force of friction opposes its motion.

3. Pile a number of heavy books on a table. Place one end of a bar magnet under the top book, as shown in Figure 11.

4. Tie one end of a piece of thread to a paper clip. Tape the other end to the table. The magnet should be strong enough to keep the paper clip suspended as shown.

5. Cut the lower end of the thread with scissors. You'll see the paper clip "fly" to the magnet.

What's Going On?

The potential energy between the two magnets changes to kinetic energy when you release one of the magnets. The same is true of the magnet and paper clip when you cut the thread.

Keep Exploring—If You Have More Time!

- With the paper clip floating below the magnet, determine through which materials the magnetic field can act. Put different thin materials between the magnet and the paper clip. Try cardboard, paper, plastic, aluminum foil, glass, a tin can lid, a saucer, a water-filled saucer, a cookie tin, and coins.

    Through which materials can the magnetic field pass? Which materials block the magnetic field? Can you "cut" the field above the paper clip with scissors? Try it!

- Can you create potential energy using the opposite poles (N and S) of two magnets? Can you convert the potential energy to kinetic energy?

bar magnet

thread

Figure 11. You can set up a paper clip and magnet as shown, and then change potential energy into kinetic energy when you cut the thread.

12 Changing Light to Electricity

What's the Plan?

Let's find a way to change light energy to electrical energy.

What You Do

1. Place a solar cell in bright sunlight.

2. Use two wires to connect the leads from the solar cell to a milliammeter (Figure 12).

3. Let sunlight fall on the solar cell. You will see the meter indicate that an electric current is flowing. (If the needle turns the wrong way, reverse the connections to the meter. If the needle then goes off scale, cover part of the solar cell.)

WHAT YOU NEED:

- silicon solar cell

- milliammeter
  (This meter can measure thousandths of an ampere.)

- 2 connecting wires with alligator clips
  (These first 3 items can be purchased at an electronics store.)

- sunlight

4. Use your hand to cover more and then less of the solar cell's surface. You will see that increasing the area exposed to sunlight produces more electrical energy.

5. Turn the cell to change the angle at which sunlight strikes the cell. Change it slowly from 90 degrees to 0 degrees. You can see that the electrical energy decreases as the angle to the sun changes from 90° to 0°.

What's Going On?

Solar cells, like those found on roofs, can change light energy into electrical energy.

Keep Exploring—If You Have More Time!

- Use solar cells to run a toy electric motor.

- Investigate the possibility of installing solar panels on the roof of your home or school.

- Show how sunlight can be used to heat water.

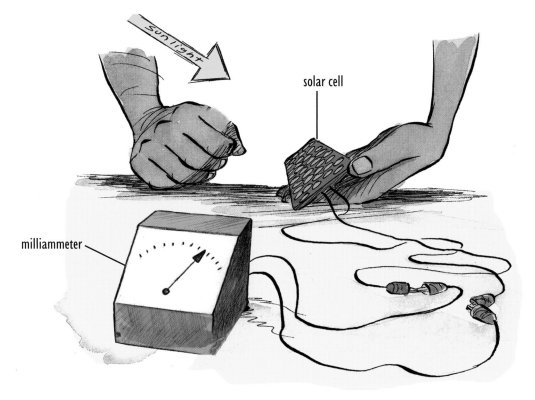

Figure 12. Converting the energy in sunlight to electrical energy

13 Contraction and Expansion of a Liquid

What's the Plan?

Let's see how adding and removing heat affect the volume of a liquid.

What You Do

1. Fill a narrow-neck bottle to the brim with very hot water. Be sure it is completely filled.

2. Carefully place the bottle in a pan of cold water (Figure 13a). Wait five to ten minutes.

3. While you're waiting, put your finger on the bulb of a thermometer (Figure 13b). Watch the liquid expand.

4. Return to the bottle of hot water. You will find that the water level has fallen as the water has lost heat energy.

5. Nearly fill the same bottle with cold water.

6. Put the bottle in a pan of water. Under adult supervision, place the pan on a stove and heat the water. You will see the water level rise as it gains heat.

What's Going On?

Liquids shrink slightly as they lose heat. They expand slightly when heat is added. When a liquid is heated, its molecules move faster and take up slightly more space. When a liquid loses heat, its molecules move slower and take up slightly less space.

Keep Exploring—If You Have More Time!

- Does a gas expand when heated and shrink when cooled? To find out, pull the neck of a balloon over the mouth of a 1-L soda bottle. Let hot tap water run over the bottle. Does the gas (air) expand? Put the bottle in a refrigerator. Does the gas shrink when cooled?

- Do other gases, such as carbon dioxide, behave in the same way? Do experiments to find out.

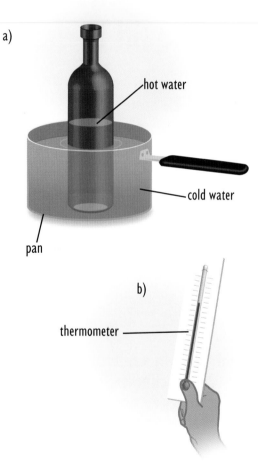

Figure 13. a) Fill a narrow-neck bottle with hot water. Place the bottle in a pan of cold water. b) Put your finger on the bulb of a thermometer.

5 Minutes or Less

Are you desperate? Do you have very little time to prepare a project? If so, you have come to the right place. Here are energy experiments you can do in five minutes or less.

14 Using Energy to Change a Solid to a Liquid to a Gas

What's the Plan?

Let's use energy to change ice to a liquid and then the water to a gas (steam).

What You Do

1. Find a one-gallon, clear, plastic bag that can be sealed. Put an ice cube in the bag.

2. Remove air from the bag by flattening it. Then seal the bag so nothing can get out.

3. Place the bag in a microwave oven (Figure 14). Have an adult turn on the oven. Watch what happens through the window.

4. Watch as the ice melts and becomes liquid water.

5. Watch the volume increase as the water boils and becomes a gas. When the bag is full, stop heating.

WHAT YOU NEED:

- an adult
- ice cube
- one-gallon, clear, plastic bag that can be sealed
- microwave oven

6. Keep the oven closed for several minutes. Watch the volume shrink as the gas condenses back to liquid water.

What's Going On?

Energy supplied by the oven changed ice to water and then water to steam. Once the heat was removed, the gaseous water cooled and condensed back to liquid water.

Keep Exploring—If You Have More Time!

- Under adult supervision, design and do an experiment to find out how much heat is needed to change one gram of water to steam at the boiling point (100°C or 212°F).

- Icicles form when snow melts and drips off a roof. How can water freeze, forming icicles, when the temperature is warm enough to melt snow?

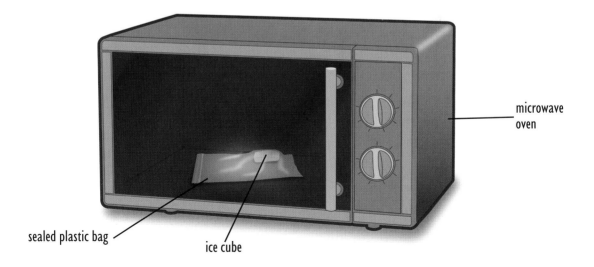

microwave oven

sealed plastic bag

ice cube

Figure 14. What happens when energy is added to an ice cube in a closed space (a sealed plastic bag)?

15 Energy from Electric Lights

What's the Plan?

Let's test incandescent and fluorescent lightbulbs to see which type is more efficient.

What You Do

1. Find a fluorescent and an incandescent lightbulb that have about the same wattage.

2. Put the bulbs in sockets side-by-side. Ask an adult to connect both bulbs to electrical outlets.

3. Hold your hands near (not touching) each lightbulb (Figure 15). Notice that the incandescent bulb produces more heat and less light than the fluorescent bulb.

WHAT YOU NEED:

- an adult
- 2 light sockets
- fluorescent lightbulb and incandescent lightbulb with approximately the same wattage
- electrical outlets

What's Going On?

The fluorescent bulb is more energy efficient than the incandescent bulb. Given the same electrical power (wattage, which is energy per second), the fluorescent bulb produces more light and less heat than the incandescent bulb.

All forms of energy can be changed to heat. Unless you are interested in heating something, energy in the form of heat is energy wasted. In this experiment, you compared fluorescent and incandescent lightbulbs. Both produce light and heat, but the incandescent lightbulb wastes more energy as heat rather than light.

Keep Exploring—If You Have More Time!

- On a lightbulb, you will find its wattage written. A watt is a measure of power (energy per second). A kilowatt is 1,000 watts. Power companies measure energy in kilowatt-hours (kilowatts x hours used). From an electric bill, find out how much your power company charges for one kilowatt-hour. Then determine how long the lightbulb is on each month and estimate the cost of its use.

- One horsepower equals 746 watts or 550 foot-pounds per second. Do an experiment to measure a person's horsepower. Can you find anyone who can work like a horse?

fluorescent lightbulb

incandescent lightbulb

Figure 15. Fluorescent and incandescent lightbulbs both produce light energy. Which one is more efficient (produces more light and less heat per watt)?

16 Watching Energy Changes

What's the Plan?

Let's watch the changes in energy when a falling mass stretches a spring.

What You Do

1. Hang a spring from a fixed hook.

2. Attach a one-kilogram mass or a plastic pail containing one liter of water to the lower end of the spring (Figure 16a).

3. Hold the mass so that the spring is at its natural (unstretched) length.

4. Release the mass. Watch it fall to a low point, stretching the spring, and then rise again to very nearly its original height (Figure 16b).

WHAT YOU NEED:

• spring that increases in length by 20 to 25 cm when a 1-kg mass hangs on it

• firm hook or nail

• 1-kg mass or a plastic pail containing one liter of water (1.0 L of water weighs 1.0 kg)

What's Going On?

As the mass falls, it loses the potential energy it had due to gravity (PEG) while gaining kinetic (motion) energy and transferring elastic potential energy (EPE) to the spring. Kinetic energy reaches its maximum at the midpoint. When the mass reaches its lowest point, there is no kinetic energy (it stops momentarily); all the lost PEG has been changed to EPE. As it rises, it gains kinetic energy, again reaching a maximum at the midpoint, while EPE is being converted back to PEG. At the top, most of its PEG has been regained, there is no kinetic energy, and the EPE is minimal. This can go on until all motion stops. The mass will then hang from the midpoint with no kinetic

energy, some EPE stored in the spring, and some PEG relative to the lowest point. Any energy less than the original PEG will be thermal energy in the spring and air.

Keep Exploring—If You Have More Time!

- Will a rubber band and small masses, such as heavy steel washers, behave like a kilogram mass on a spring?

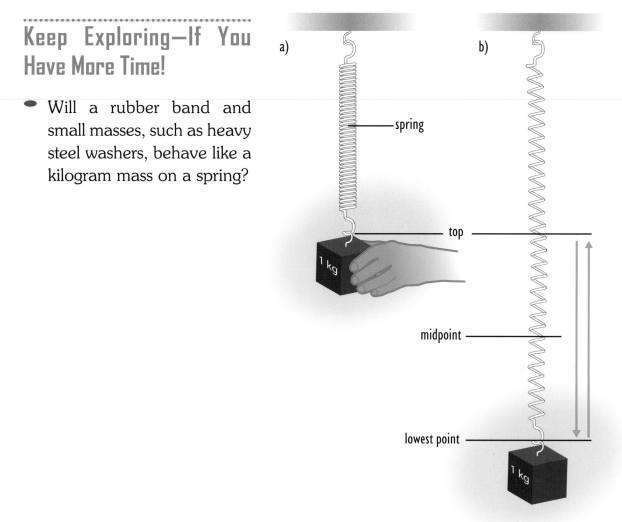

Figure 16. a) An unstretched spring with held mass ready to fall b) A stretched spring and mass after the mass has fallen to its lowest point

17 Doing Work Can Produce Heat

What's the Plan?

Let's see how doing work can produce thermal energy (heat). Remember that work is a force acting through a distance (W = F x D).

WHAT YOU NEED:

• large flat rubber band about 1/4 inch wide

What You Do

1. Hold an unstretched rubber band against your forehead (Figure 17a). It should feel cool.

2. Hold a short section of the rubber band between your thumbs and index fingers (Figure 17b).

3. Do some work on the rubber by stretching the section between your thumbs and index fingers (Figure 17c).

4. Immediately after stretching the rubber, hold the stretched section against your forehead. It should feel warm.

What's Going On?

When you stretched the rubber, you did work on it. The molecules in the rubber gained some kinetic energy because of the work you did on them. That molecular kinetic energy appears as thermal energy.

Keep Exploring—If You Have More Time!

- You can also generate heat by doing work on your hands. Rub your hands together rapidly and forcibly. You will feel them become warm.

- You may have heard that Native Americans, who did not have access to matches, started fires by rubbing two sticks together. Under adult supervision, investigate how a fire can be ignited by doing work on sticks. Is a particular type of wood required?

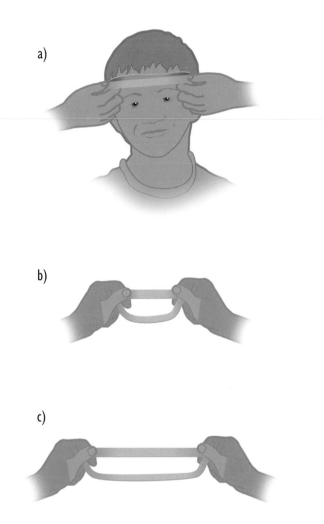

a)

b)

c)

Figure 17. a) Hold a rubber band against your forehead. b) Hold a short section of the rubber band between the thumbs and index fingers of your two hands. c) Stretch the rubber as far as you can. Then hold the stretched rubber against your forehead.

18 Energy Lost or Conserved in Collisions

What's the Plan

Let's see what happens when different kinds of balls collide with a smooth concrete floor.

WHAT YOU NEED:

- Super Ball™
- smooth concrete floor
- tennis or a golf ball
- ball of clay

What You Do

1. Drop a Super Ball™ onto a smooth floor. You will see the ball rise to nearly the height from which it fell (Figure 18a).

2. Drop a tennis or golf ball onto the same floor. It will bounce, but not as high.

3. Mold some clay into a ball. Drop the ball onto the concrete floor. It simply flattens and does not bounce at all (Figure 18b).

What's Going On

These collisions are between a ball and the earth (the concrete floor is firmly fixed to the earth). A perfectly elastic collision is one in which no kinetic (motion) energy is lost. A totally inelastic collision is one in which all the kinetic energy is lost.

The collision of the Super Ball™ was very nearly an elastic collision. The collision of the clay was an inelastic collision because it lost all its kinetic energy. The collision of the tennis or golf ball was partially elastic; it lost, perhaps, half of its kinetic energy. Of course, if you let any of these balls continue to bounce, they will eventually lose all their kinetic energy and come to rest. The lost kinetic energy will have changed to thermal (heat) energy.

Collisions between gas molecules or between the molecules and the walls of their container are perfectly elastic.

Keep Exploring—If You Have More Time!

- Are billiard ball collisions nearly elastic?

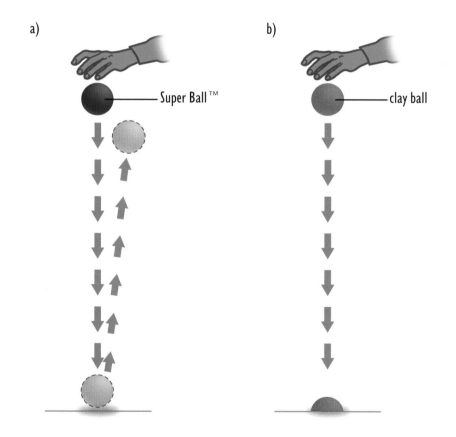

a)   b)

Super Ball™   clay ball

Figure 18. a) The collision between a Super Ball™ and the earth is almost an elastic collision. **b)** The collision between a clay ball and the earth is an inelastic collision.

Words to Know

calorie—The heat energy needed to raise the temperature of one gram (1 g) of water one degree Celsius (1°C).

elastic collision—A collision between two objects in which no kinetic energy is lost. Such collisions occur only between molecules or atoms.

elastic potential energy—The energy stored in a stretched object such as a spring or rubber band.

energy—The capacity to do work.

expansion caused by heat (thermal expansion)—An increase in size caused by the addition of thermal energy (heat).

fluorescent lightbulb—An energy efficient lightbulb that emits light generated by a fluorescent material coated on the inside of the bulb.

heat (thermal) conduction—The movement of thermal (heat) energy through a substance.

heat conductors—Substances that conduct heat well.

heat insulators—Substances that do not conduct heat well.

incandescent lightbulb—A lightbulb that produces light by heating a filament to a high temperature.

immersion heater—An electrical device that can be placed within a liquid and used to heat it.

inelastic collision—A collision in which there is a loss of some or all of the initial kinetic energy possessed by the colliding bodies.

kinetic energy—The energy associated with motion, which is equal to half the object's mass times its velocity squared ($1/2\ mv^2$).

pendulum—An elongated body, often a weight on a string, that is free to swing back and forth as it is pulled by gravity.

potential energy—The energy related to the position of a body, as in a raised mass that can fall when gravity does work on it. See also elastic potential energy (EPE) and chemical potential energy.

power—The rate at which work is done.

watt—A unit of power equal to 0.24 calorie per second or 1 joule per second.

wattage—The electrical power (number of watts) required to operate an electrical appliance, such as an immersion heater.

work—The product of a force times the distance through which the force acts (W = F x D).

Further Reading

Books

Bardhan-Quallen, Sudipta. *Championship Science Fair Projects: 100 Sure-to-Win Experiments.* New York: Sterling, 2007.

Muschal, Frank. *Energy from Wind, Sun, and Tides.* Ann Arbor, Mich.: Cherry Lake, 2008.

Nardo, Don. *Kinetic Energy: The Energy of Motion.* Minneapolis, Minn.: Compass Point Books, 2008.

Ollhoff, Jim. *Solar Power.* Edina, Minn.: ABDO Publishers, 2010.

Oxlade, Chris. *Energy.* Mankato, Minn.: Smart Apple Media, 2009.

Plummer, Todd. *I've Discovered Energy.* Tarrytown, N.Y.: Marshall Cavendish Benchmark, 2008.

Reynoldson, Fiona. *Understanding Solar Power.* New York: Gareth Stevens Publishers, 2010.

Rhatigan, Joe, and Rain Newcomb. *Prize-Winning Science Fair Projects for Curious Kids.* New York: Lark Books, 2006.

Slade, Suzanne. *What Can We Do About the Energy Crisis?* New York: PowerKids Press, 2010

Internet Addresses

Super Science Fair Projects Ideas, Topics & Experiments
http://www.super-science-fair-projects.com

What Is Energy?
http://www.eia.doe.gov/kids/energyfacts/sources/whatsenergy.html

Index